The Forgotten Friend

Gary Richmond

Illustrated by Bruce Day

WORD PUBLISHING

Dallas · London · Vancouver · Melbourne

VIEW FROM THE ZOO STORIES are based on the real-life adventures of Gary Richmond, a veteran of the Los Angeles Zoo, minister, counselor, and camp nature speaker. Gary has three children and lives in Chino Hills, California, with his wife, Carol.

The Forgotten Friend
Copyright © 1991 by Gary Richmond for the text.
Copyright © 1991 by Bruce Day for the illustrations.

Library of Congress Cataloging-in-Publication Data

Richmond, Gary, 1944-
    The forgotten friend//Gary Richmond; illustrated by
    Bruce Day.
    p. cm.
    Summary: Ladybug, a black and tan puppy, teaches
forgiveness and friendship in a happy reunion.
    ISBN 0-8499-0913-9
    [1. Dogs–Fiction. 2. Friendship–Fiction. 3. Christian
Life–Fiction.] I. Day, Bruce, ill. II. Title.
PZ7.R413Fo 1991
[Fic]–dc20   91-21400
                                          CIP
                                          AC

Printed in the United States of America

1 2 3 4 5 6 9 LBM 9 8 7 6 5 4 3 2 1

This book is dedicated to Kenneth Crosley, my special friend forever.

Hi, I'm Gary Richmond, and I'm a zoo keeper. As a zoo keeper, I've learned a lot about God's wonderful animals. At the same time, I've learned a lot about God.

This true story is about my family's dog named Ladybug and a lesson in friendship and forgiveness.

When I was seven Ladybug came to live with us. She was a small black-and-tan puppy. I don't remember where we got her. But I do remember the warmth of her head lying across my bare feet. And I remember love in her eyes as she hoped to be invited on adventures outside of our yard.

Ladybug loved to ride in the car. She would lean out the back window of our station wagon. The wind would whip her ears and flap her lips. No dog ever enjoyed anything more.

Ladybug weighed about fifteen pounds. And she was probably part cocker spaniel and part beagle. No one knew for sure.

A happy dog, Ladybug was ticklish. If you scratched her in just the right place, she actually smiled. I know that's hard to believe. But, if you saw it, you would say she smiled, too.

I thought of Ladybug as a member of the family—the youngest child. She slept with us and licked me awake. I never had to wash my ears because Ladybug did it for me every morning.

Ladybug was my friend and shadow. I always loved her but never more than when I had to ask for her forgiveness.

It was a hot August day. We were out of school. And I had a little extra money. I remembered how much I enjoyed biting into one of old Mr. Kern's great dill pickles at the delicatessen. So, I asked my friend, Doug Sigler, to walk to Kern's with me. My older brother Steve and a friend of his decided to go, too.

When we got to the front door, Ladybug was wiggling with delight. She was sure that we were going to let her come along. We finally agreed and went out the door together.

Ladybug was not leashed because she would never bite anyone. She was always running just ahead of us. She would stop now and then to smell something and make a memory. Then she would run over and jump up on us. She was letting us know how glad she was to be part of the adventure.

When we arrived at Kern's, we told Ladybug to sit at the front door. She had to wait for us while we went inside to eat. I bought one piece of pumpernickel bread, one slice of aged Swiss cheese, one large dill pickle, and a bottle of Dad's Old Fashioned Root Beer. Nothing was better than that! Licking our fingers clean at last, we left.

Once we were outside, we called Ladybug to follow us home. Twenty steps down the street, we came to Hillcrest Pharmacy. In the window we saw the new issue of *Mad Magazine*.

Again we told Ladybug to sit on the sidewalk and wait for us. And we went into the store.

We all read the funny magazine over Doug's shoulder. And we laughed at the silly jokes.

Finally, the store clerk asked us to buy the magazine or leave. So, we left . . . through the back door. It was a shortcut home.

We forgot Ladybug was waiting patiently at the front door of the pharmacy for us.

Afternoon soon became evening. Our friends both left for their homes and dinner. My dad came home from a hard day of work. He was a builder. After washing up, he called us to the dinner table. It was a meat-and-potatoes dinner—the kind with lots of leftovers that Ladybug loved. My dad scraped them onto a plate and stepped out the back door to call Ladybug.

She didn't come. So, he asked Steve and me if we had seen her. We looked at each other, both suddenly knowing what we had done. I didn't answer. I hoped Steve would answer first and get most of the blame for losing Ladybug. At last Steve told Dad that we had left her outside Hillcrest Pharmacy.

My dad had a disappointed look, which he aimed at both of us. He told us to jump in the car, and we did. We backed out of our driveway a lot faster than usual. Dad didn't say much. But he did ask if we had traded our brains for sawdust. At the time, it seemed like a fair question.

Dad knew that Ladybug could follow her own scent home. So, he followed the route we had walked to the delicatessen. The farther we drove without seeing her, the worse I felt. I had let down my best friend, and I knew it. I had a lump in my throat. What if she had been run over by a car? What if she was in a cage at the dog pound?

We finally turned the corner at Mariposa Lane and Lake Street. There was a small dark form curled into a ball by the front door of the pharmacy. I was so happy! Steve stuck his head out the window and yelled, "Here, girl."

His yell awoke her. She jumped up against the glass
of the pharmacy. She thought we were still inside the
store. That made me feel awful again. Steve got out of the
car and picked her up.

It was a happy time for all of us. Ladybug wiggled until I thought she would fall apart. She whined all the way home. And she licked every hand that came within a foot of her.

That night I asked Ladybug to sleep with me. Her tail
wagged as she ran ahead of me and jumped up on the bed.
When I turned out the light, I called her to come closer.
Then I hugged her tight. I told her how sorry I was to have
let her down. She just gave me a big, sloppy, doggy kiss
and rolled over for me to scratch her tummy. That was her
way of saying, "I forgive you." I scratched her until we
both fell asleep.

Ladybug was always ready to forgive. All she wanted was to be part of our family, her family. The saying that a dog is a man's best friend is surely true of Ladybug and me.

Sometimes I think about the time I let Ladybug down. And I think about how she forgave me. Then I remember Jesus.

One of His closest friends let Him down, too. When Jesus got into trouble, Peter pretended that he didn't even know Him (John 18:15-18, 25-27). He acted as if he had forgotten Jesus, just as I forgot Ladybug. When Peter realized what he had done, he felt terrible, just like me. He was so upset with himself that he cried.

The Bible says that Jesus is our very best friend in all the world. But we all let Him down sometimes. Then it says the most wonderful thing of all—Jesus loves us so much that He forgives us. Even when we don't deserve it, Jesus forgives us. And He wants us to forgive others the same way, too. I guess Ladybug must have learned that lesson somewhere. I just hope I can learn to be forgiving, too, when someone hurts me.

Isn't forgiveness wonderful?